IN THE NAME OF GOD

Entrepreneurship as done by

Hossein Sahiholnasab

The Founder of
Sahiholnasab Construction Group

Written by:
Dr. Reza Yadegari
Dr. Mahshid Sanaeefard
The Winners of the Prestigious
Jalal Al-e Ahmad Literary Award
and
Aryaan Yadegari
Lilyaan Yadegari
The Second Generation Authors of the
Great Iranian Entrepreneur Book Collection

Serial Number: P2446190216
Title: Entrepreneurship as done by Hossein Sahiholnasab
Subtitle: The Founder of Sahiholnasab Construction Group
Authors: Dr. Reza Yadegari & Dr.Mahshid Sanaeefard
Co-Authors: Aryaan Yadegari & Lilyaan Yadegari
ISBN: 978-1-77892-141-4
Metadata: Biography & Entrepreneurship
Book Size: Paperback
Pages: 66
Canada Publish Date: September 2024
Publisher: Kidsocado Publishing House

Copyright @ 2024 By Kidsocado Publishing House
All Rights Reserved, including the right of production in whole or in part in any form.

Kidsocado Publishing house
Vancouver, Canada

Phone: +1 (833) 633 8654
WhatsApp: +1 (236) 333 7248
Email: info@kidsocado.com
https://kidsocado.com

- **Introduction**   3
- **The Greenlight**   5
- **The life and world of Hossein Sahiholnasab**   7
- **The analysis of the founder of Sahiholnasab Construction Group**   39

Introduction

The work of identifying the greatest Iranian entrepreneurs got underway back in 1997 with the help and assistance of my wife Dr. Mahshid Sanaeefard, the Manager of the Great Iranian Entrepreneurs Publication. An exceptionally long and arduous task, which has enabled us to gain substantial insight into the world of entrepreneurship and job creation, and thus make history for the future generation of Iranians by helping found and chart a whole new path towards true success in business and industry alike.

Next to winning numerous international awards on this incredible journey of countless ups and downs, we have cooperated and collaborated extensively with some of Iran's highly accredited and most reputable higher learning centers, like Sharif Industrial University, University of Science and Technology, Alzahra University and Shahid Beheshti University. Moreover, we have also successfully established and registered the International Qualification and Certification Auditors Company or IQCA in Canada, whose main role and responsibility is to publish the life history of the greatest Iranian entrepreneurs to make them known by name to the other people in the world. IQCA has also been highly active in setting up and establishing an award presentation scheme in Iran in order to identify and introduce the country's most creative individuals and organizations, and thereby aid and assist with promoting them on a global scale.

It is hoped that as a special and leading group, we are able to introduce the most powerful Iranian women and me to the rest of the world and at the same time, identify and retell the life stories of the best role models for Iran's next generation.

Dr. Reza Yadegari
www.UNESCO.ws

The Greenlight

The movement to transfer the experiences of the world's greatest entrepreneurs is one of the most important factors in helping the American and European companies and organizations' progress and improvement. These companies and organizations had concluded rather smartly that if a society wishes significant advancement and development, it must keep its eye on the experiences of the previous generation and not allow the young to incur costs on the system by experiencing and learning through trial and error. In line with the same notion, entrepreneurship has the potential to create notable transformation throughout a given society's various levels provided it is implemented using principles and plans that take advantage of the experiences of the proficient and skilled members. Allowing the young to take over across the world is certainly a commendable measure, which has also been taken in our beloved Iran as well, except that here the experiences of the previous generation of entrepreneurs and managers has never been made properly available for application by the new generation – something that has regrettably inflicted irrecoverable costs onto the country because of the continuous repetition of the same old mistakes. Our project to identify the greatest Iranian entrepreneurs, so that we may research their lives to understand the reasons and factors for their success started off back in 1997 simultaneously as the arrival of the novel science of entrepreneurship in Iran. Admittedly, the path has been a long one involving strenuous effort. In the years following the events of the Iranian Revolution, literary no entrepreneur in the country was willing to unveil and reveal herself or himself and the experiences she or he possessed.

In spite of this, we were quite determined to fulfil our goal of teaching and training the future generation by documenting and publishing the life stories and experiences of Iran's greatest entrepreneurs through a one-thousand-volume book aptly titled 'Entrepreneurship as done by …' What is presented in the book collection, is rare and valuable roadmap designed based on the experiences and performances of Iran's greatest economic minds, which undoubtedly can be a wonderful asset in guiding and directing anyone who intends to get involved in any type of commercial, production and service provision activity. We hope that our collection book can help open up doors and pave the way for Iran's new generation of young entrepreneurs, and also remain a lasting piece of literary work to remember us by.

Dr. Reza Yadegari
Dr. Mahshid Sanaeefard
Tehran, Iran 2024

The life and world of
Hossein Sahiholnasab

My Childhood

I was born in 1933 in a large family in the village of Khalilabad, Taft. I was the fourth child in the family, following my brothers, Seyyed Kazem and Seyyed Ali, and my sister, Robabeh Sadat. Two more daughters joined the family after me, making me the youngest son. This position brought me extra affection from my siblings and parents, especially my mother. From a young age, she allowed me to sit by her prayer rug, joining her in worship and devotion. I must admit that my habit of praying punctually, no matter the circumstances, is a legacy from my devout and loving mother, who taught us to love all beings and to live as true humans. She was not only a loving mother but also a supportive partner to my father, working side by side to ensure our comfort and well-being.

My father was a hardworking and humble man. If I describe him as humble, it's because throughout his life, he focused entirely on his work and avoided gossip and prying into others' lives. Instead of competing with fellow villagers, he concentrated on his own trade and worked tirelessly, much like my mother, to provide us with a relatively comfortable life. He was a farmer and also raised a few livestock. Occasionally, he would work as a camel herder, taking six or seven camels to pasture while surveying the desert and grazing lands. I remember once, four of his camels went missing, and he spent two whole days searching the desert. When he returned to the village, he found that the camels had found their way back home before him.

Our village, Khalilabad, lies between Taft and Yazd, closer to Taft and considered part of its outskirts. The distance from Khalilabad to Yazd is about three Farsakhs (Persian unit, about 20 kilometers), which we children often walked to reach Yazd, and a quarter of that distance to reach Taft. Today, thanks to modern transportation, it takes less than twenty minutes to travel from Khalilabad to Yazd and five minutes to Taft.

In Khalilabad, we didn't have a school, and only a few families could afford to send their children to the city for education. Our financial situation didn't allow my father to send us to school. We weren't poor, but we had no extra money; our income only covered our basic needs. A few years later, a school was established in our village, but by then, I was over twelve years old and not allowed to attend. I learned to read and write in adult literacy classes and from the village's Quran teacher, village's Mullah. My father taught me arithmetic, using an old wooden abacus that I remember well.

Starting from the age of five, I became proficient in financial matters. I was a sharp and nimble child, quick-witted, and good at talking to people. Even as a child, people recognized my strong interpersonal skills.

Back then, our village had no vehicles or even enough horses and donkeys for transportation. Elderly villagers couldn't walk the distance to Taft to buy cigarettes and tobacco, so we children would run the five kilometers to Taft, make the purchases, and quickly return to deliver the goods. Besides this, I also sold small items like sewing supplies to the village women, contributing to my family's income.

Before I turned twelve, I supported myself and partly my family through these small jobs. Summers brought the unbearable heat of the desert, while winters were harsh with heavy snow, making travel conditions extremely challenging. You might be surprised to learn that I endured the severe winters of the desert region in Yazd, but due to the proximity of Mount Shirkooh, the area experienced bitterly cold winters. Particularly in the village of Sakhoid, we witnessed exceptional snowfall and freezing temperatures.

Sakhoid, a neighboring village of ours and part of the Taft district, has a history stretching back 1,500 years. The early inhabitants of Sakhoid, like those in other parts of Yazd, were Zoroastrians. Over time, due to the harsh climate and heavy snowfall, they migrated away, leaving behind remnants such as fire temples and tombs. Today, however, thanks to the efforts of various development sectors, Sakhoid has become a prominent winter sports destination, with its ski resort attracting many visitors for skiing and snow activities. Despite the absence of enough ski equipment there, a few locals rent out tubes for sliding down the slopes, adding to the fun of playing in the snow. On the mountain's steeper parts, it's uncommon to see a tube reach the bottom without its riders tumbling and rolling. However, these thrilling moments—soaring through the air, rolling in the snow, and experiencing the excitement and spills—seem to encourage others to try this exhilarating activity at least once.

A painful memory from when I was sixteen haunts me: a pregnant woman died along with her unborn child because the snow blocked the way to the city. I promised myself that if I ever became wealthy, I would build a clinic in this region before even considering a school.

Moving to Tehran

I always dreamed of doing great things and despised aimless work. I stayed in the village with my family until I was twelve. My older brother, Seyyed Ali, had moved to Tehran for work in construction with some relatives. When he returned after a year, he got our parents' permission to take me with him to work as a laborer in Tehran. Leaving my childhood memories behind, I set out for Tehran. My family was worried about the separation, but I believed that my prosperous future lay in the big city. Though I knew that everyone's sustenance is guaranteed by the Creator, I felt confident that I would shine brightly in this vast city and make my parents proud.

For a boy my age, Tehran was like an endless ocean. More than its diverse people, I was fascinated by its grand architecture and sturdy buildings. Coming from a place where the architecture reflected ancient Iranian designs, I was awed by the massive iron and concrete structures in the capital.

I worked as an assistant to my brother and other builders, handing them bricks and making mortar. This was a far cry from my self-reliant childhood, but I didn't want to remain a wage-earner forever. We lived in a half-finished room at the construction site. On weekends, I eagerly visited my mother's aunt in Tehran, who washed my clothes and treated me to her delicious cooking.

After more than a year of labor, I began to learn construction techniques by observing contractors and architects. At fifteen, after finishing my work, I would go to the market near the Shrine of Abdul Azim and help build arched roofs, using my knowledge of traditional methods from the desert region.

I spent my earnings on necessities, sending most of my daily wages back to my family in Khalilabad. I wanted my family, especially my father, to live comfortably. There were times when employers delayed or even withheld our wages. I remember working for a high-ranking colonel who refused to pay us. Unable to complain formally, we waited at his house every day, hoping to get paid. One day, two brothers loudly cursed the colonel and were beaten by his henchmen. A painter, trying to impress the colonel, also kicked one of the brothers. The brother cursed the painter, and shortly after, the painter injured his eye. This incident taught me that one must always act justly, for the consequences of one's actions will inevitably follow.

Another lesson came when I was repairing a poorly built house.

The elderly mother of the homeowner, while praying, cursed the original builder, saying, "May his soul suffer as this house shakes." This made me realize the importance of doing quality work, as people's blessings or curses are eternal.

Becoming an Architect

For a year and a half, I worked alongside my brother and other relatives as a laborer. But, as I mentioned before, I constantly watched the contractors and architects, trying to learn from them. I wanted to become independent as soon as possible and work for myself. I often told my older brother, "This isn't real work. A person should work for themselves, not for others!"

Seyed Ali Agha would laugh mockingly and say, "Focus on your work, kid, and stop aiming too high."

One day, along with a relative known as "Master Ahmad," we took on a contract to build a wall around a large piece of land. In construction terms, taking a contract means managing a project. On the last day, after finishing the work, we went to the employer for payment. The employer gave us half the money and offered a piece of land in Yaftabad as the remaining payment. Master Ahmad took the cash, and the land was given to me instead of the rest of the wages. A year later, I sold that land for thirteen times its original price and bought a larger piece of land in another area, intending to build a house for myself.

For three months, every Friday evening after work and before going to the Abdolazim Bazaar, I would visit my land, sit on the half-built wall, and stare at the land in front of me, dreaming of how I would develop it. In that small plot of land, I imagined a grand mansion, a luxury home as they would call it today. The house I envisioned was entirely different from and better than anything I had built in the past year and a half. It was a stylish, unique house that would captivate any buyer.

After a few months, I decided to bring my dream to life and build my property. I reached an agreement with the builders and workers I knew, and they agreed to help me with the project. When my brother found out, he scolded me and mockingly said, "You think you've grown up too fast. Stay in your place, kid. Building a house isn't for everyone; it takes a strong person." He then ordered me to stop this "nonsense" and return to working under him. But I was determined. I told him, "I don't want to be someone else's worker forever. I want to be a builder and do things myself."

Seeing my determination, my brother tore up the land contract and left me alone with my land and dreams. I rolled up my sleeves and started building. With the help of friends, relatives, and even Master Ahmad, who had initially hesitated to accept the land, we laid the foundation of the building. I immediately went to the landowner and told him, "I've lost the land contract. Can we draft and exchange a new official contract?"

A few months later, through day and night effort, I completed my first house. I built it with great style and taste, creating something beyond the typical structures in the area. Everyone who saw the house fell in love with it, and many buyers wanted it. I sold the house at a very good price, and the money became the capital for my future construction projects.

After succeeding in this venture, my older brother recognized me as an independent architect and builder. He joined me in future projects, and within the same year, I built and sold eighteen houses.

Despite my young age, my strong social skills made all the builders and workers loyal to me, and they put their hearts into the work. I, in turn, made sure to pay them promptly and fairly, never delaying or neglecting their wages. I was also very frugal and economically minded. I neither gave away money freely nor took it without earning it.

Even though I never went to school, I learned architectural principles through experience. I taught myself traditional drafting and set up a room in my house as an office, where I drew the plans for all the buildings I constructed. I tried to understand everything related to construction and mastered the principles of architecture. I collected all the magazines and photos related to architecture and consulted many architects and contractors. Whenever I saw a project or a partially built structure, I would immediately approach the architect or head designer to learn from their experience.

Gradually, the name Sahiholnasab and the beautiful buildings I designed became known to everyone. Just hearing that a building was designed and built by Hossein Sahiholnasab made people eager to buy it. I became a well-known architect at a young age, and everyone wanted a house designed by me. My name and reputation became my brand.

I built six or seven-story buildings on Mir Emad Street, all highly sought after. I constructed a very beautiful and luxurious building on Takht-e Tavoos Street, which even Mohammad Reza Pahlavi considered for his office. When a colonel came to purchase the property and secure the contract, I said, "If the Shah, the country's first person, doesn't pay me, who should I complain to?"

I never worked for a company; I always worked for myself. I designed and built homes and estates for many prominent figures.

I also invested in Yazd and the city of Taft, designing and building homes for many of the region's elite. I even built the Philco and Philver refrigerator factories in Yazd. Later, they entrusted me with the construction of Plastiran factory, Yazd Baft factory, and Rangin paint factory.

When I arrived in the Khalilabad and Sokhoid regions, it was time to fulfill a promise I had made to myself. I immediately established a clinic on a ten-thousand-square-meter piece of land the government had provided near Shirkooh, where that pregnant woman and her baby had died from the cold and snowstorm years ago. The clinic was fully equipped with medical and dental facilities, exceeding my expectations. I also built two small residential units for doctors and planted walnut and almond trees around the clinic, allowing the staff to cover some of the clinic's expenses by selling agricultural products. I later purchased an ambulance for the clinic. Today, this clinic is recognized as one of the model healthcare centers in the region.

Marriage and Family Formation

In 1955, I got married and settled in Tehran. My first child, Hamid, was born in 1957. After him, God blessed my wife and me with five more sons—Davoud, Ali Mohammad, Naser, Vahid, and Amir—and a daughter named Afsaneh Sadat, who completed our happiness. I felt honored to lead my large family.

When Hamid was six, I asked him if he could write the word "account." He struggled a bit but managed to put the letters together on paper. I told him, "Well done! From today, you're my accountant." Hamid showed an interest in architecture at the age of seven, helped me with drawing plans and making models at ten, and at thirteen, he built a ceramic model valued at $8,000. I involved all my sons in the construction and accounting world from a young age so they'd understand that money isn't easily earned and that serious effort is required to succeed in life.

I remember once haggling over a taxi fare with a driver. Hamid and Davoud were with me, and they said, "Dad, you're wealthy. Why haggle over a few cents?" I replied, "Because I want you to learn the value of negotiation. We neither take money for free nor give it away unnecessarily."

By the mid-1960s, the demand for constructing six or seven-story apartments in Tehran was rising. I participated in these projects both as a contractor and independently. Soon, I established my own construction office on Mir Emad Street, from where I managed all my orders and planning. The buildings I constructed were unique in terms of materials, architecture, and structure, and they were sold quickly after completion.

I progressed faster in my career than anyone, including myself, had imagined. After selling each house, customers who knew me and had bought from me would greet me warmly whenever they saw me, saying, "Our prayers are always with you and your team." Hearing such words and achieving customer satisfaction was the greatest reward for me.

I always tried to lead by example in charitable activities, setting a standard for my children and society.

During the Shah's time, there was an initiative for philanthropists to build dormitories for university students in Tehran. At the time, construction had just begun on dormitories in Amirabad (the current University City), but the project was halted due to a lack of funding. Mr. Mohammad Taghi Rasoulian approached me and said, "Sahiholnasab, why don't you build the dormitory for the people of Yazd?" I immediately agreed and said, "Let's start. You can break ground for the Yazd dormitory." He replied, "We can't; Prime Minister Hoveyda has to do it." But at the insistence of the people of Yazd, I went ahead and started the construction. I was able to complete and hand over the building to Mr. Rasoulian before anyone else could finish theirs. The Yazd dormitory was the only one with a prayer room; others lacked this facility, so students had to pray in their rooms.

Another charitable project I fondly remember is the construction of the "Imam Zaman Mosque" at the corner of Behboudi and Azadi streets. The mosque had been left unfinished for many years, and no architect had been able to complete it. The

Shah had issued an urgent order: finish the construction quickly or demolish it, as it was an eyesore for foreign dignitaries driving past from Mehrabad Airport on Eisenhower Avenue (now Azadi Street). I stepped in and told the contractor and the board of trustees, "You haven't been able to complete this mosque in years. Give me the authority to build it. I'll do it with my own money and resources. I'll fund the first year myself and offer a meal during Ramadan at this mosque. Then I'll announce the costs, and the board of trustees will cover part of the expenses so I can continue construction the following year." They accepted my terms, and I took over the project. I enlisted the best architects and builders from Yazd and completed the mosque in the beautiful style of Yazd architecture. For two consecutive years, I provided meals at the mosque during Ramadan for the board and caretakers. In the third year, one of the caretakers called me, saying, "Mr. Sahiholnasab, we were expecting an invitation for this year's Ramadan meal at your mosque, but it seems there's no event this time?" I replied, "Where have you been? I finished the mosque in the second year and handed it over to the board of trustees. I even covered the last 300 tomans from my pocket." Everyone involved, including many from the royal court, were amazed at our swift work and the mosque's exquisite design.

I also owned a 600,000-square-meter plot of land in Karaj with my Yazdi partners. We sold it in shares to several government employees. I personally fenced the land, planted trees, and parceled it out in 2,000-square-meter plots for the customers.

When the engineers and municipal employees from various districts, who knew me to some extent, arrived to receive their land and gardens, they were surprised to see each other and asked, "When did you buy this land?" They all answered, "From Sahiholnasab." Some immediately contacted me, saying, "Mr. Sahiholnasab, why didn't you tell us our colleagues also bought land here?" I replied, "Sorry, you are friends and colleagues, yet you didn't inform each other about your purchases. How could I share others' private affairs with you?" Working with people over the years taught me not to say anything unnecessary. When something needs to be said, the person involved will speak up. I've passed this wisdom on to my children, advising them never to be bearers of other people's words.

Building Student Dormitories and Mosques

During the Shah's era, there was a call for philanthropists to build dormitories for Tehran University students. Construction had just begun on the Amirabad dormitories (current University of Tehran dormitories) but was halted due to a lack of funds. Mr. Mohammad Taghi Rasoulian, who was in charge, approached me and said, "Sahiholnasab, please build the Yazdi dormitory." I immediately accepted and said, "In the name of God, you lay the first stone for the Yazdi dormitory." He replied, "We can't; Prime Minister Hoveyda must come and lay the first stone." Before Hoveyda could arrive, at the insistence of the Yazdis, I laid the first stone myself and completed the construction quickly, handing it over to Mr. Rasoulian. The Yazdi dormitory was the only one with a prayer room, unlike others where students had to pray next to their rooms.

Another charitable project I fondly remember is the construction of the "Imam Zaman Mosque" at the corner of Behboodi and Azadi streets. The mosque had been left unfinished for years, and no architect could complete it. The Shah had issued an urgent order to either complete its construction promptly or demolish it entirely. The sight of this unfinished grand structure was unpleasant for political dignitaries and foreign leaders passing by after leaving Mehrabad Airport via Azadi Street (formerly Eisenhower Street). I intervened, telling the contractor and the board, "You couldn't advance the mosque's construction in these years. Give me the mandate to build it. I'll fund the first year myself, host an Iftar here next Ramadan, disclose my expenses, and then you, the board of trustees, will fund part of it. I'll continue the construction until the next Ramadan." They agreed, and I took on the project. I invited the most skilled Yazdi architects and builders to collaborate and constructed the mosque in the beautiful Yazd architectural style. For two consecutive years, I hosted Iftar in the mosque. In the third Ramadan, a trustee called me, saying, "Mr. Sahiholnasab, we were waiting for your Iftar invitation this year, but it seems there's no Iftar?" I replied, "Brother, where have you been? I completed and handed over the mosque to the board in the second year. I even paid the final three hundred tomans from my pocket." Everyone involved in the mosque's construction, including many courtiers, were astounded by our speed and the unique architecture.

Revolution of 1980 and the Iran-Iraq War

As I mentioned earlier, I introduced my son Hamid and his brothers to the world of construction and accounting from a young age. Before the 1980 Iranian Revolution and the subsequent significant changes in the country, Hamid and Davood, in particular, accompanied me in construction work. I would take them to project sites and teach them the tricks of the trade. Sometimes, I would deliberately bring accounting books and building plans home and ask Hamid and Davood to go through the accounts and report back to me.

A few years before the revolution, television and its programs had become popular, and most people would rush home early in the evenings to watch their favorite shows. While watching TV, Hamid and Davood would also review my accounts. They would be half-focused on the TV and half on calculating. Although I knew they would make mistakes in their calculations and percentages, I allowed them the opportunity to correct their errors. Late at night, when they returned the audit book, I would leave it on my desk on purpose, where they could easily access it. I often saw them sneaking into my room after their favorite show, taking the audit book upstairs, correcting their mistakes, and returning it to my desk. They knew they were dealing with a strict father who never compromised on work.

I always had a close relationship with my children and tried to provide the best for them. As Davood once said, "Whenever I think back to my youth, I can't remember a single night when Dad came home without a shopping bag." He was right. Every week, I would come home with a new and fashionable outfit. My teenage sons, eager to get their hands on the clothes, would say, "Dad, this style doesn't suit you!" I would immediately reply, "Well, I bought it for you to wear."

In my opinion, one should always want the best for their family—eating the best food, wearing the best clothes, and living a happy life in the best home with their loved ones.

Along with being a friend to my children, I also taught them the principles of business. For example, whenever my children needed more pocket money than usual, I would tell them they could earn it by washing my cars. I would pay ten rials for washing the big Chevrolet Caprice and five rials for the BMW 2002. Most of the time, Hamid and Davood, my older sons, were responsible for washing the cars. Later, I found out that Hamid had hired the gardener, Mostafa, to wash the cars while he supervised, earning fifteen rials from me and only paying Mostafa five rials, thus making a profit without doing the work himself.

I also paid them for other chores like vacuuming the house, washing windows, and helping with the dishes, providing assistance to my late wife, Nosrat. This way, I tried to teach my children the value of money from a young age. My fourth son, Naser, often accompanied his mother to the Tajrish market for household shopping. His mother would buy ice cream for him and his siblings. One day, when Naser asked for ice cream but his mother said she only had enough money left for the taxi fare, she suggested he buy ice cream with his own money. Naser replied, "We don't spend our hard-earned money on food."

From the age of 12 or 13, Hamid was responsible for accounting for my projects. Every night, after finishing his schoolwork, he would spend an hour writing up the expenses for my projects. This kept him involved in my work and gave him valuable experience in managing construction projects.

In 1976, Hamid graduated from high school and entered university, majoring in Business and Computer Science. However, he was more interested in architecture and planned to serve in the military before studying architecture in the United States. Around the same time, he received an acceptance letter from the University of Maryland, College Park, for studying architecture. Without delay, I sent him to pursue his passion. A few months before this, I had sent my third son, Ali Mohammad, to a boarding school in Virginia. Following Hamid, I sent Davood and Naser to the United States for their studies, effectively sending four of my sons abroad within a year. I visited them occasionally and made sure they were doing well. Although I provided them with enough money for their needs, they were determined to work alongside their studies.

Each of my sons chose a field related to construction, as they wanted to establish a construction company together. Hamid studied architecture, Davood specialized in structural engineering, Ali Mohammad focused on mechanical engineering and construction management, and Naser decided to complete his studies in electrical engineering.

In the U.S., they all worked, despite receiving adequate financial support from me. They had been raised to never rely solely on their father's money. Initially, they delivered newspapers, cycling around and dropping off newspapers at homes. This job earned them green cards sooner than expected, as their work was considered legal. Later, they started driving rental cars, picking them up from hotels or residences and returning them to the airport. Because of their high-speed driving, I often worried and reminded them to be careful.

I frequently traveled between Iran and the U.S. and, a few months before the 1979 revolution, I became involved in a significant construction project on Shah Abbas Street in Tehran. However, the revolution caused the investor to leave the country, and the project was halted and seized by the revolutionary forces.

My two youngest sons, Amir and Vahid, were only about 12 or 13 years old when I reluctantly sent them to the U.S. to join their brothers, hoping they would all study and grow together. The separation from our six sons was tough for my wife, Mrs. Nosrat Pilevar, and me, especially since she had been by my side through all of life's hardships. We made a pact not to send our only daughter, Afsaneh Sadat, to the U.S. for her studies.

During those years, when even making a phone call abroad was challenging, Afsaneh Sadat's presence was a comfort to us, especially to her mother. She helped me with some business and banking tasks and, like her brothers, was eager to pursue higher education. Although we didn't send her to the U.S. for her studies, she continued her education in Iran, eventually earning a degree in psychology.

Two years later, when I went to Maryland to settle Amir and Vahid, I discovered that Hamid and his brothers had started building beautiful homes for the local Iranian community. I was delighted and proud of them. It seemed that construction was in their blood. Hamid explained how they had gotten involved in construction:

"One day, an Iranian contacted me and said over the phone, 'A friend of mine wants to build a house and would like some information about column diameter, wall thickness, ceiling height, and so on.' I told him, 'You can't build a house over the phone; I need to see him in person.' When I met the man, I could tell from his tone and questions that he wasn't willing to pay much and wanted to build his house cheaply. However, he had seven plots of land, making it worthwhile to invest in the project. Remembering the lessons you taught me, I offered to build the first house for him for free. I told him, 'If you sell it and make a good profit, you'll give me the other houses to build, and I'll charge you for them.' We agreed. My brothers, who were busy buying and selling cars at the time, helped with the design and supervision. The house turned out so stylish and beautiful that even before it was finished, the owner sold it for a 200% profit. Overjoyed, he asked us to design and oversee his other houses, and since then, we've designed 60 houses for him."

I was over the moon with pride and happiness, eager for my

sons to finish their studies and return to serve their country. None of them served in the military; instead, I legally purchased their military exemption so they could continue their studies. I remember the day I went to the conscription office to buy my third son's military exemption. The staff there said, "Someone here holds the record for buying the military exemption for four sons." Jokingly, I replied, "Wait, I'll break the record soon." And I did. Not long after, I bought the exemptions for my fifth and sixth sons and set the record.

During the Iran-Iraq war, the construction business, like many other industries, slowed down. The economic pressures after the revolution, the war, and sometimes unstable management in the real estate market, along with the involvement of various institutions in buying and selling land, caused many problems. Few people dared to invest their savings in housing during such uncertain times, with cities under constant threat of bombardment.

However, I should note that during the early years of the Islamic Revolution, when many people lost their properties and there was no clear plan for housing, the Supreme Leader issued a decree for "Account 100" to help provide housing for the needy. The activities of this account included providing financial assistance for housing expenses, building affordable and durable housing through donations, and assisting tenants with rental deposits through no-interest loans. As a result, the Housing Foundation of the Islamic Revolution was established to help build and provide housing for low-income groups. It has since built many residential units and has helped rebuild homes destroyed by natural disasters like floods and earthquakes.

Meanwhile, I continued to follow up on my children's academic progress and register their documents with the Ministry of Science. I supported my family through small construction projects, but I was happy knowing my sons were progressing in the U.S. as skilled architects and builders. They had decided to gain experience and earn money through construction while studying.

Hamid and his brothers established an architectural and construction company called HDA. They initially entered the market by buying and selling land, and soon after, they started designing and building houses. I had high hopes that they would use the experience they gained abroad to help rebuild Iran after the war. It was their sense of duty and love for their country that encouraged them to return. But alas, this did not happen, and they were instead persuaded by the other side to settle in Canada. While I am proud of their accomplishments and success, I wish they had returned to serve their homeland, especially since I raised them with this expectation.

Mrs. Nosrat Pilevar, my devoted wife, passed away in the winter of 1995. She had suffered from stomach cancer, which had metastasized to her lungs. This was a significant blow to me and my family, and we were devastated by her loss. I buried her in the family plot in Behesht-e Zahra cemetery, where I visit her grave every year.

With all my children now living abroad, I continued my construction work in Iran, though my heart was heavy with the weight of their absence. I remain hopeful that one day they will return to their homeland, bringing their skills and experience to help build a better future for Iran.

Return of the Sons to Iran

In 1992, three of my sons returned to Iran. Vahid and Amir had to stay longer in Maryland because they were studying medicine. When Davood came back to Iran, a year before Hamid, Ali Mohammad, and Nasser, my daughter Afsaneh Sadat had already been married for a year and had recently given birth. The arrival of our first grandchild brought new joy and vitality to the lives of my wife and me, who had endured years of separation from our children. Davood also decided to get married and start his own family. He joined me in my work, settling into life in Iran. After my sons returned, I decided to retire and leave all construction matters to them. However, before stepping back completely, I needed to share my full knowledge and experience with these young, educated engineers. Additionally, they had to prove their abilities and skills to me, their father, before entering the world of construction in Iran.

For their first project, I gave them my villa in Zaferaniyeh. They were to demolish it and build a chic and modern nine-unit building in its place. The boys were on the verge of marriage and starting families, which motivated them to complete the project quickly.

Throughout the construction of this building, I taught my sons everything I had learned and experienced over the years. Once the building was finished and they settled in with their families, I bought another piece of land and handed it over to them. I told them, "You must handle this project on your own, without my help, because I don't want people to say that my sons rely on their father's support."

I can say that the competition in construction and the housing price surge started right after the end of the Iran-Iraq War, around 1989. As the economy began to recover after an eight-year hiatus, the housing market experienced a price boom in the early 1990s. Many property owners took advantage of this by rebuilding their houses and constructing six- or seven-story buildings. This trend led to a rise in newly built residential units and an increase in migration from rural areas to big cities.

It was in this environment that my sons entered the construction industry. Before retiring and handing over all responsibilities to them, I advised them, "Remember, our work isn't seasonal. Always prioritize integrity and kindness. People are aware of who works honestly and conscientiously, and only this energy of honesty and integrity will reach them."

When I bought the Mir Damad office for them, I planned to retire and leave everything to the boys. However, they asked me to continue as an advisor and supporter, allocating 20% of the shares of each building and property to me. I thank God that, with patience and without greed, my sons and I have always pursued our work. They have made me proud, leveraging both academic knowledge and the practical experience I've shared with them. They have excelled in each project, surpassing their previous achievements.

After returning to Iran, they established the Hands Company, known for its high-quality buildings, the best materials, the latest construction technologies, unique architectural designs, and long-term guarantees. They have successfully designed, supervised, and executed over 150 projects in Iran. Some notable projects include the luxury residential "Behesht Tower" in Zaferaniyeh, the villa complex "Behesht Darya" in Kelarabad, Mazandaran, the residential towers "Shirkooh," "Sasan," and "Mehran." Additionally, their successful "Galleria" shopping center and office building was opened in winter 2016.

If I were to summarize my sons' work, I would say that, beyond being a supportive father and a traditional architect, their primary concern has been to create flawless buildings that blend the qualities of Iranian architecture with the contemporary needs of Iranian society.

Principles of Architecture and Construction Experience:

Before delving into the principles of architecture and our work methods, I want to remind readers, especially the younger generation, of the fundamental principles that apply to any profession. As I mentioned earlier in my memories, honesty and integrity are crucial in our work. Make sure not to bring ill-gotten gains into your life. Always work with a clear conscience so that others' blessings will follow you.

Once, I experienced living in a house that trembled every time a truck passed by due to the negligence and lack of care from its builder. The elderly owner would curse the architect every day while praying. That experience was a wake-up call for me; I promised myself always to do my work properly and meticulously because people's prayers or curses can change your destiny. From that day on, I knew that as an architect and builder, I needed to supervise every detail, no matter how small, like applying window putty, and never overlook them.

A few years ago, while crossing the pedestrian bridge in Abbas Abad, an elderly man approached me. After a moment of recognition, he asked, "Aren't you Mr. Sahiholnasab?" I replied, "Yes, that's me. How can I help you?" He quickly kissed my shoulder and said, "I bought one of the five units in Argentina Square from you about twenty-seven or twenty-eight years ago, and even after all these years, my house has never leaked, and I've never had to replace the asphalt."

Another time, a young man came to my sons' office and said, "Because my father bought one of the five units in Argentina Square from your father over thirty years ago and was very satisfied, I want to buy a unit from your company for myself."

Always keep three key factors in mind for your projects:

1. Draw good plans in your design.
2. Spend wisely; don't cut corners on building materials, from the structure to the foundation.
3. Have a strong work ethic.

Don't seek fame; work with passion. Let your reputation be your brand, not just your name.

I often tell young people who come to our company for work: if you have the money and opportunity to continue your education, do so and enter this profession with knowledge and expertise. But if you don't have the money, come to me; I'll pay for your university, but you must work on the projects and follow the work from start to finish with precision. You must start learning carefully and gradually. I ask them if they want to be an architect or a builder. You can be both with your academic knowledge, or like me, who became a builder through experience, you can become proficient in all aspects of the profession with patience and perseverance.

You must always update your knowledge and attend conferences, seminars, and workshops. I didn't have a university education, but by observing closely, listening carefully, and working conscientiously, I could establish this company and brand.

Today, the name "Sahiholnasab" is more recognized than the "Hands" company, and despite having multiple companies and a specific logo, our family name has become the main brand and source of our reputation.

Currently, we don't engage in turnkey contracts unless specific materials are unavailable. We don't subcontract to builders and installers because we prioritize quality over quantity. We tell our builders and architects, "Today, whether you work three meters, two meters, or even one meter, what matters to us is the quality of your work, not the speed."

Work should not be seasonal. Like all professions, construction has its ups and downs and can experience fluctuations and recessions. But if you approach your work thoughtfully and avoid greed, you will always succeed. A job, like raising a child, requires care and attention.

We never enter into a construction contract without ensuring the land and property are sound. We choose clean, trouble-free land for construction. If we're invited to a house with problematic property, we decline the invitation.

In my opinion, a young engineer who graduates from university should experience the entire construction process, from excavation to painting and landscaping. We tell our trainees to be present even during the demolition of old buildings, as it's very instructive. With their involvement in the first project, they become a junior builder. In the next project, they can become an assistant architect, and if they act responsibly and appropriately, they can lead the project in the third one. If they excel at this stage, the investor won't let them go and will want to partner with them on all projects.

On the other hand, we've also experienced cases where a young engineer worked with us for nearly ten years but remained at the same skill level as in the second year and never grew. Why? Because they had no passion for the work and were only there to collect a paycheck.

Many have used our brand to gain credibility for themselves and take on prestigious projects under the "Sahiholnasab" name without our knowledge. For example, a person who interned with us for six months participated in a few sessions and projects, took souvenir photos with us, and then went to another company. They showed the pictures and, based on their brief time with us, managed to secure the lead on a major tower project. I'm more surprised at how the investor or client trusted this intern and gave them the project without even calling us to verify their claims. While I admire the young person's resourcefulness, any technical issues will first damage their reputation and then our company's name and brand.

Today, few are unaware of the goals and vision of the Sahiholnasab Engineering Group. We consider ourselves pioneers in designing and constructing buildings over the past few decades, with our main concern being to provide flawless buildings that blend the essence of Iranian architecture with contemporary societal needs.

The Path to Success from the Perspective of Hossein Sahiholnasab

I believe more in the journey to success than in the secret to success. My message is particularly for the young people who are entering the workforce and the world of competition. As students, you should seek knowledge. We live in the age of the internet, where information and knowledge are exchanged at lightning speed. This era is vastly different from my time and even from the time of my children, thirty or forty years ago. Today, you can find everything on the internet. Unlike the past, you don't need to travel to the ends of the earth to advance. Now, with the click of a button, you can stay updated on the latest developments in architecture and construction from anywhere in the world.

Most of my grandchildren, except for six, completed their education in Iran, unlike their fathers who went to the United States for further studies. They have become skilled engineers and architects and are now working here in Iran. Last year, several of my grandchildren collaborated and won third place in the group category for public buildings, from design to execution, at the 13th Iranian Architecture and Interior Architecture Award. They earned this recognition for designing and constructing "Grandpa's Kitchen," a building that seamlessly blends traditional and modern architecture in my hometown, Khalilabad Taft, Yazd, and stands out as a gem in the region.

I believe Iran has the potential for growth in all areas, especially the construction industry, provided we all work conscientiously and with integrity, relying on God and supporting each other.

Everywhere in the world has its unique challenges, and "the sky is blue everywhere." If today we face difficult conditions while acquiring knowledge and making a living, there have been similar struggles in other parts of the world at different times. Unfortunately, today's youth have become quite impatient. They want to achieve a hundred years of progress overnight, but much patience is needed to mature. One of the fundamental conditions for success in personal and social life is self-management. People should seek the root of all success within themselves. A successful person is one who never gives up trying, no matter the circumstances, and never compromises on their goals. After every dark night comes a bright morning of hope and victory.

To reach your dreams anywhere in the world, you must work hard. If you can endure the hardships with patience and perseverance without veering off course, you will undoubtedly reach the peak of success and your dreams. Once you succeed, you will rarely face obstacles that can hold you back, and you will soar upward like a rocket.

Another important point is to always take the initiative in charitable deeds and never hesitate to help others. If you encounter someone in need, know that your meeting is not accidental. Be aware that God has a plan for both of you; He tests your heart as a supporter and the other person's heart as a receiver. Give without expecting anything in return and be as generous as you can. I've experienced the truth of the saying, "Do good and throw it in the Tigris; God will return it to you in the desert," throughout my life. I fully believe in it.

I remember years before the revolution, it was mandatory for young people, after completing high school, to serve as "Knowledge Corps" members, promoting literacy in remote villages and towns instead of doing military service. A person who came to Khalilabad Taft, our village, for this service dreamt of studying in Germany after his service. However, he lacked the financial means and was very distressed about it. Although I had never attended school, I encouraged him to pursue his studies in Germany, promising to cover his education expenses. Without even asking his name, I provided him with the funds for his education and travel. To this day, I do not know his name or what he is doing in Germany.

But I am happy and filled with love for my Creator because I know He has always watched over me and supported me and my family. I constantly remind my children of one thing: "Always take the lead in charitable works." Whenever you're asked for help with building schools, clinics, purchasing dowries, or funding education and university, don't turn away. As the saying goes, "Whenever you can, throw a pea into the pot."

Final Words

My final words are that everything I have, I owe to the blessings of my parents. Since childhood, I always gave my earnings to my parents. Their comfort and well-being were my life's priority. As long as they were alive, my main salary was theirs, and I only kept the overtime pay for myself. My mother constantly prayed for me, saying, "May whatever you touch turn to gold," and "May your children be the light of your heart." It was her blessings that have ensured I never faced a "no" in my work and emerged successful from every project.

In addition to the blessings of your parents, which I hope always guide you, I want to share twelve points with you; young people; that will help you achieve your goals and succeed in your business, ensuring you never feel disappointed or disheartened:

1. Focus on your commitment, not your motivation.
2. Seek knowledge, not just results.
3. Distance yourself from discouraging thoughts.
4. Work and strive continuously.
5. Don't be overly lenient with yourself.

6. Eliminate distractions.
7. Maintain a healthy and active lifestyle.
8. Plan your activities.
9. Never retire yourself early; Alzheimer's can strike if you do.
10. Always set goals.
11. Make the best use of your time.
12. Show genuine respect to receive genuine respect.

On the importance of the last point, respect, I want to emphasize that genuine respect comes from the heart. Let's strive to love everyone sincerely and show respect to both young and old. By respecting our younger ones, we spend our time innovating for them, which brings joy to our hearts and pleases God, making our world more peaceful and happier.

Every day, I pray to gain God's love and serve those He deemed worthy of creation. I urge all of you, including my sons, to work together to prosper and elevate this land. Unity, unity, unity. You can easily break one pencil, but no one can break seven pencils bound together.

Analysis of Success Factors of the Founder of
Sahiholnasab Construction Group

When we look at ordinary lives, we see that some people have achieved remarkable success while others continue to live in regular circumstances. This disparity often raises questions about why some individuals end up on certain paths while others do not. Fortunately, the study of success has developed to address these questions effectively.

The truth is, our lives are composed of repetitive actions and thoughts. We repeat various tasks and ideas throughout the day. According to psychological principles, each repetition either increases or decreases its effect. Repeated actions or thoughts can strengthen over time, much like a thread wound around us. Initially, these threads can be easily broken, but as they accumulate, they become stronger and more difficult to break. Eventually, these repeated actions and thoughts form habits that shape our behaviors and character.

Understanding these repetitions is crucial for analyzing the lives of successful and unsuccessful individuals. What do successful people repeat daily, weekly, monthly, and yearly? How do these repetitions transform into habits that ultimately lead to success or failure? By focusing on these points, we can discern why some people achieve success, some achieve great success, and others remain ordinary.

Interestingly, if we can identify and compile the repetitive behaviors of successful people, we can develop a rich understanding of success. This knowledge can then be managed, categorized, and shared. When others read and repeat these behaviors, they should theoretically achieve similar results, unless they encounter issues in implementation that require correction. The field of success literature has emerged with this approach, leading to a significant increase in self-made millionaires over the past century.

Success principles can be identified and categorized in any country. The fundamental rules of repetition and overcoming challenges may vary across different cultures and geographies. In Iran, for instance, analyzing the lives of successful individuals has become prevalent, leading to the creation of a uniquely Iranian success literature. By identifying the repetitive behaviors in the professional, business, and financial lives of successful Iranians, we can understand the causes of their success or failure and categorize them for broader use. Success is simpler than one might think. As Brian Tracy notes, if you know what successful people in your field do, and you repeat those actions, you will achieve similar results. Tracy was astonished by the simplicity of this idea when he first realized it. He would ask successful people about their practices, emulate them, and find success.

You don't need to seek out such people yourself. Books like the one you are reading can easily inform you of these behaviors and repetitions. By repeating these behaviors, you can achieve outstanding results. Isn't that a straightforward path to success? Seyed Hossein Sahiholnasab is one of those individuals who has created a reputable brand and name for himself. If you aspire to achieve similar recognition in various fields, you can simply study his life to understand the path he took and the outcomes he achieved. By reading this book and identifying the factors behind his success, you can replicate them and reach great heights. As one highly successful individual remarked, he simply understood why others succeeded, identified their actions, and then did those things two or three times more intensively. If successful people were early risers, he would get up even earlier. If they were avid readers, he would read twice as much. By reading books like this and intensifying these behaviors, your success is guaranteed.

Hard Work

Let's talk about one of the key principles of success in the workplace and organizations. These methods are also applicable in various other fields and can propel you forward. If you intend to work in companies and organizations, you only need to do two things:

First, work harder. Arrive at work earlier in the morning, spend less time on lunch, work more, stay later in the evening, and maintain greater focus and intensity.

Second, ask your employers and managers for more responsibilities. Initially, this request might not be met with approval. However, over time, your willingness will be noticed by your employers and managers, and they will turn to you when needed. When that time comes, apply the first principle diligently.

Conclusion

By studying the life of Seyed Hossein Sahiholnasab and understanding the behaviors that led to his success, you can adopt and intensify these actions to ensure your own success. Whether it's working harder or seeking more responsibilities, the key lies in consistent, focused effort and the willingness to go above and beyond. Follow these principles, and you too can achieve great success in your endeavors.

The Principle That Matters

By following these guidelines, you can easily continue your progress and achieve great success. However, the principle that stands out most prominently here is the principle of hard work. This principle can propel you forward, though it might not always lead to direct results. Still, it will undoubtedly contribute to your success. Essentially, you move forward by exerting maximum effort. While these efforts might not always yield the desired results, they will lead to other unexpected outcomes. These unexpected successes often arise from the diligence you put in, opening doors you hadn't anticipated. This is why hard work, as Steve Jobs famously said, is half the reason behind the success of great entrepreneurs—what he referred to as sheer perseverance.

Success in Unexpected Places

To clarify, for success in business and economics, you must be hardworking. However, hard work alone will not suffice. It is necessary for progress but not sufficient by itself. Being hardworking, combined with other traits, will advance you. Without hard work, even with other essential qualities, you will not get far. While it's incorrect to attribute everything to hard work, it is crucial to have this habit alongside traits like intelligence, creativity, human engineering, opportunity recognition, staying updated, and high knowledge to achieve remarkable success.

A Real-Life Example

Reviewing the life of Seyed Hossein Sahiholnasab exemplifies this point well. He was hardworking even as a teenager, working until 5 PM and sending all his earnings to his family. He would then work extra hours until midnight to support himself. Remarkably, he managed multiple projects simultaneously, often to the astonishment of those around him. He would even sleep on sand at night to continue his work the next morning, just like an ordinary laborer. This level of perseverance is rare and noteworthy.

The Essence of Perseverance

Pure perseverance is a treasure to be seized whenever found. Whether in sports, culture, art, business, or economics, this trait is exceptionally valuable. One famous bodybuilder referred to previous bodybuilders as having immense perseverance, citing examples of individuals who trained so hard that their mouths would foam, or whose screams under heavy weights would echo through the gym. Despite the hardships, they never retreated and achieved the highest ranks in their fields. Such is the nature of pure perseverance.

Accessible Role Models

To achieve notable success in your field, you should look up to individuals like Sahiholnasab as models of determination and success. These people managed several large projects simultaneously and never shied away from challenges. Are you willing to sleep on sand to advance your project? Are you prepared to defy expectations and prove your perseverance to others? As Kim Woo Choong, founder of the renowned Daewoo Corporation, said, no significant success comes from half-hearted efforts. If your efforts are tentative, you won't achieve great success. But if your efforts are hard, intense, and focused, significant successes will come your way. Success comes from intense focus and hard work, not from any other path. Arriving late to work, lacking focused effort, spending excessive time on lunch, and constantly engaging in irrelevant conversations with colleagues will not make you successful. Roll up your sleeves, embrace hard, intense, and focused efforts, and success will follow. These efforts might seem daunting at first, but once you overcome the inertia of inaction and begin moving, things will progress more smoothly. Are you ready for such intense and focused efforts? Then great success is waiting for you.

High Financial Knowledge

In his books, Robert Kiyosaki introduces new financial concepts. He points out that today's economy is not like the traditional economy of the past, which is necessary. We face a modern economy. However, he also emphasizes reinterpreting old economic concepts in new ways, which can significantly aid you in your journey.

From Traditional to Modern Economy

We all have a particular view of assets, thinking everything we own counts as our assets. This is true in traditional economics, where debts, income, and savings have specific definitions. However, modern economics defines assets differently: an asset is something that affects your income. For instance, your job affects your income, but owning a property that generates rent also adds to your income, thus becoming an asset.

While it seems obvious that real estate is an asset, the distinction in modern economics is that only income-generating real estate counts as an asset. Owning multiple properties that do not contribute to your income does not make them assets. Even if property prices increase due to inflation, it doesn't equate to income. Selling these properties to buy new ones or invest elsewhere still requires accounting for the new inflation rate. Thus, what seems like an asset in traditional terms may not hold in modern economics.

Real Assets

If we consider assets as something that generates income, then what are real assets? In reality, properties can be real assets if they generate rental income for you. If you own stocks that yield dividends, you have real assets. If you own machinery or equipment that you can rent out for money, these are also real assets. If you have made investments that earn you money without your direct involvement, these investments are your real assets. Additionally, if you have published a book or built a brand and earn royalties from them, these can also be considered real assets. These concepts, if well understood in modern economics, can be utilized to generate income and profit. As Jim Rohn said, "When you earn, you can live; but when you profit, you can achieve wealth."

A Great Lesson from Seyed Hossein Sahiholnasab

Seyed Hossein Sahiholnasab offers an interesting perspective on this new concept of assets. He says that if you build a place just to sleep in, it's a loss. This aligns with what Robert Kiyosaki emphasizes. Imagine you have a fifty-billion-toman house but live in it. Is this property an asset? It might be better to call it a potential asset; you can convert it into cash whenever you decide. But even this cash is not inherently valuable unless you increase it. Kiyosaki suggests that financial intelligence today involves acquiring assets and using them to acquire more assets, essentially turning one into two and two into three, and so on. From the income of one asset, you gain another, and from the income of the first and second assets, you acquire a third. This process ultimately leads to financial independence. If you live off your savings or initial capital, it will eventually deplete. But if you live off the income from serial investments, you'll never run out of money. This is the essence of modern assets, a concept many people do not understand, still working and saving in outdated ways.

A Lesson for Everyone

This significant lesson from Sahiholnasab is particularly valuable for those in real estate and construction. They shouldn't just build and hold; they should generate profit through building and selling. If they need to hold properties during market fluctuations, they should ensure these properties generate income, making them real assets. These lessons are applicable to everyone, regardless of their job or financial status.

Personal Branding

Reading the life story of Seyed Hossein Sahiholnasab, you can't overlook the importance of personal branding. A significant part of his success can be attributed to his personal brand. But what is personal branding?

Personal branding is essentially about managing the intersection of individuals and their expertise. It differentiates people within the same field, making them stand out. Personal branding is about marketing an individual's skills and services to gain recognition and, consequently, increase income and opportunities.

An Important Point

Personal branding isn't about false advertising. You need skills, experience, and a suitable personality to build a strong personal brand. Investing in non-existent qualities is futile. To enhance your personal brand, focus on the skill-experience-personality triangle and ensure everything is genuine. Personal branding influences how others perceive you, creating a distinct identity among peers and competitors. If done correctly, your brand becomes an asset. Consider influencers— their fame and brand are their assets, and others pay to associate with them, unlike us, whose reputation doesn't require such payments. This is why public figures and athletes often have brand managers to maintain their image.

Remembering Napoleon Hill and Dale Carnegie

Napoleon Hill first introduced concepts akin to personal branding in his famous book "Think and Grow Rich." Hill, often regarded as the father of success literature, identified this important concept early on. Similarly, Dale Carnegie, another pioneer in the field, contributed valuable insights into personal influence and branding.

The Core Mission of Personal Branding

The core mission of a personal brand is to evoke specific thoughts and feelings in the minds of the target audience. Everyone has a personal brand, as our actions or inactions create impressions. If no impression is made, it means their personal brand is non-existent. Thus, behaviors and actions—or the lack thereof—affect the growth or decline of our personal brand. To strengthen your personal brand, begin with self-awareness, understanding your daily actions, words, and even thoughts. Without this self-awareness, you cannot improve. Once you understand your current brand, determine what changes are needed to create or refine your desired brand. Then, consistently practice these behaviors and attitudes until they become habits. This process will develop your unique personality, distinguishing you from others in your field.

Why Should We Market Ourselves?

The question often arises: if we do our job well, why do we need personal marketing to become recognized and credible? Many people cite the famous example of Mercedes-Benz, arguing that it doesn't need marketing because its quality speaks for itself. But the main question is, did a brand like Mercedes-Benz achieve these positive associations overnight? The truth is that these associations are the result of years of consistent quality, which has become ingrained in the company's culture, and today, it benefits from this reputation.

However, more important points are:

1. Who Knows About Your Work? How many people know that you do your job well or exceptionally? Sit down and count the approximate number of such people. You will likely find that you have a small target audience. With a small audience, you won't achieve significant success. Therefore, you need a larger audience that can spread the word about you and create special opportunities for you.

2. Do Others Also Excel in Your Field? Are you sure others in your field are not doing their jobs well? Just as others might not know about your excellent work, you might not be aware of theirs. This means you are in a competitive environment, and other factors will contribute to your success.

What Do Others Know About You?

This brings us to a crucial point in our business, especially if it is organizational, corporate, or governmental: hard work alone is necessary but not sufficient. As mentioned earlier, you must add other qualities to yourself, your business, and your personality. Simply working hard with your head down is not enough; you need to create the right associations in the minds of others and your target audience. The Entrepreneurship Journal has written an article highlighting interesting points, some of which we will review:

• "Late this summer, British writer Kate Lister reached a widely echoed conclusion. She wrote on Twitter: How old were you when you realized that your primary plan to be a really good

person, work hard, and push yourself beyond normal limits, hoping for automatic rewards, was just a myth?"
• "Jeff Shannon, a career coach and author of Hard Work Is Not Enough: The Surprising Truth About Belief in Work, argues that: Hard work is a good start and can certainly help you establish yourself early in your career. But it is not enough to elevate you to the highest positions."
• "Shannon says that if no one recognizes your hard work, it doesn't matter. For your effort to lead to promotion and advancement, especially in today's changed professional world, you must ensure that people notice your efforts and that you are aware of them yourself."
• "Being at your desk before others isn't enough—you need to announce your achievements loudly."
• "Carol Frohlinger, head of the American consulting firm Negotiating Women's Issues, says that hard work still matters a lot, but waiting for someone to notice it can be harmful."
• "Frohlinger calls this tendency the 'coronation effect' (a term also mentioned by Sheryl Sandberg in her book Lean In). 'People work really hard and deliver excellent results, hoping that higher-ups will notice and crown them in appreciation. But she believes this rarely happens. One of the characteristics of people who only work well and do nothing else is that they are not visible. So, when promotion opportunities arise, no one thinks of them. They quietly and gently get forgotten.'"
• "In most companies and industries, proven ability alone is not enough to advance you. You still need to be likable and memo-

rable. Shannon says: If you want to have influence and impact, people need to trust and believe in you."
• "If you don't think about your professional position, no one else will."

The Value of Human Engineering in Your Progress

When we read and review these points, we are reminded of the famous story Dale Carnegie tells in his book How to Win Friends and Influence People: 80% of your progress, even in engineering and technical jobs, depends on human engineering, and the rest depends on your technical and specialized skills. All these points essentially relate to creating positive associations and feelings in the minds of your target audience.

Success Interpretations from Seyed Hossein Sahiholnasab's Biography

One of the significant aspects to examine in Seyed Hossein Sahiholnasab's life is his personal branding. He mentions throughout his biography that the buildings he constructed would sell before they were even completed because everyone knew that a Sahiholnasab building was of impeccable quality. He ensured there were no shortcomings in his work, which over time established his name well, leading people to buy his projects blindly. It gets even more interesting when we learn that even competitors would hire workers who had spent time working with him without hesitation, sometimes leading to misuse by some workers. However, ultimately, Sahiholnasab managed to establish his personal brand as a builder of distinctive quality.

Be Noticed for Your Uniqueness, Not for Being Showy

In the business world, it is said that to have a strong personal brand, you don't need to be conspicuous; you need to be outstanding. This simple phrase encapsulates everything we need to know. You must be among the few who can perform a task or deliver it with exceptional quality in your field. If you possess the required quality, personal branding can enhance your success. But without this quality, merely promoting yourself will lead nowhere, and sooner or later, your lack of authenticity will be exposed.

Striving for Excellence

Whether you realize it or not, you already have a personal brand in the field you've entered. You might wonder, "No one knows me for my hard work or credibility, so where is my personal brand?" Your personal brand might currently be negligible, but it exists, much like your willpower—whether it's strong or weak, it's still there. If your personal brand in your field is nearly nonexistent, what can you do? Start with small projects and tasks, completing each one with the utmost care and quality. Make it a habit to aim for excellence in everything you do. Don't just complete tasks to get them out of the way; strive to be the best at what you do. When you aim for the best, you'll naturally come up with better ideas and focus more, leading to superior results.

This approach is exactly what Sayyed Hossein Sahiholnasab took. He began by taking on small projects and doing his best work on each. Over time, his consistent excellence earned him a reputation as a top-tier builder. Until your name is well-known, you must offer your best performance. Once your name is established, protect it fiercely. As Warren Buffet said, it takes a lifetime to build a good reputation in business, but only a moment to ruin it.

The Importance of a Good Name

After years of effort to build a good name in your industry, it's this reputation that will propel you forward and open doors for you. Remember, the power of a famous name can open more doors than hundreds of books. Today, personal brands can extend beyond their initial audience. In one survey, participants were asked if they recognized the name Cristiano Ronaldo or the country of Portugal more; most said Ronaldo. This shows that a famous name can even surpass the fame of the place it originates from.

The Never-Ending Journey

Your earnings will reflect the strength of your personal brand. The law of supply and demand applies here: the less supply (people with your expertise) and the more demand, the higher you can price your services and negotiate better positions. A strong personal brand leads to more job opportunities, greater success, and better negotiating power for superior positions.

Thus, a stronger personal brand equals higher income.

Maintaining Your Personal Brand

As Sahiholnasab says, the most important aspect of personal branding is maintaining it. According to the law of inertia, if an object is in motion and no force acts on it, it will keep moving. Personal branding is similar; once established, it will continue to grow unless something disrupts it. Such disruptions could be actions or behaviors that contradict your brand. As Warren Buffet noted, you can lose a reputation built over a lifetime in a moment. Once you achieve a stable and respected personal brand, you have two major tasks: continue to enhance it and protect it fiercely.

Choosing Quality Over Quantity

Sahiholnasab highlights the importance of quality over quantity. He prefers to take on fewer projects and ensure each is of exceptional quality, rather than handling many at once with average results. This approach ensures long-term success and maintains the strength of his brand, as clients are willing to pay more for the quality they trust.

The Power of Integrity and Consistency

For those who may find the detailed aspects of personal branding overwhelming, there's a simpler approach: combining integrity with the compound effect. By consistently doing the right thing in your field, you will see results over time. As Darren Hardy describes in "The Compound Effect," consistent actions over time lead to significant differences. If you stick to good practices and maintain integrity, you'll eventually see substantial progress and success.

Doing the Right Thing Exactly Right

There's a critical distinction between doing something "almost right" and doing it "exactly right." Many people spend their lives doing things almost right, but true success comes from precise correctness. As Jim Rohn said, make sure your ladder is leaning against the right wall before you start climbing.

By understanding and implementing these principles, you can build and maintain a strong personal brand, leading to greater success and recognition in your field.

Religious Affirmations

In our religious culture, there is a principle that holds great importance in the realm of business as well. It is suggested that those who consider God in their endeavors will receive divine assistance in their worldly affairs. Simply put, if you take care of your relationship with God, He will take care of you. Other religious teachings emphasize that if your life's priority is adhering to divine commands, you need not worry about worldly matters, as God will suffice for you. Naturally, a person with true faith in God will not shortchange their work or be dishonest. Such a person is trustworthy and practices integrity.

A True Story

Allow me to share an interesting story with you. It is said that a respected scholar longed to meet Imam Mahdi (peace be upon him) in person. He prayed fervently and performed many acts of devotion, but nothing significant happened. He made vows, helped others, and followed all the recommended actions, yet he made no progress. Finally, he undertook rigorous spiritual exercises and retreats. At the end of one such retreat, he was inspired to visit a certain city, market, and shopkeeper if he wished to meet the Imam. He immediately set out to the indicated place. Upon entering the market, he found the specified shopkeeper and entered his store. Due to his spiritual exercises, he could perceive truths that others couldn't. He saw Imam Mahdi present there, sitting quietly. As he prepared to speak, the Imam instructed him to remain silent and just observe. The shopkeeper was a locksmith.

An elderly woman entered the shop, wishing to sell a lock due to financial need. The locksmith examined the lock and explained that if she wanted a key made for it, the lock would be worth a certain amount. However, if she sold it without a key, its value would be lower. He also mentioned that he needed to make a reasonable profit, so he offered her a fair price. The old woman was initially skeptical, thinking he was joking. The locksmith reassured her of the lock's true value, offering to pay her the stated amount. The woman, moved to tears, explained that she had been to several shops in the market, where others tried to exploit her need by offering very low prices. The locksmith responded, "Mother, I am a Muslim, and so are you. Why should I buy your item for less than its real value?" He paid her the fair price, and she left his shop, blessing him. At that moment, Imam Mahdi turned to the scholar and said, "Did you see? This woman visited many shops today, but everyone tried to deceive her, except this man, who upheld the principles of Islam. I visit this shopkeeper every week." Then he added, "We require nothing special from you, only that you act justly. In that case, we will come to you on our own accord."

The Result of Consistent Integrity

Do you now understand what it means to work with integrity? It is clear that anyone who adopts this method and remains consistent in their work need not worry about anything. Over time, they will naturally gain a good reputation in their field. In business, and even in personal branding, everything revolves around trust. If people learn that they can trust you blindly, you will never have to worry about your business. Blessings will continue to flow your way. This principle has been exemplified by Sahiholnasab, who has always conducted his work with integrity, believing deeply in quality and customer care. This commitment to integrity became even stronger after a significant experience: He once visited a family to see their house. A truck passed by, causing the windows of the old woman's house to rattle. She prayed, "O God, just as these windows shake with the passing of a truck, shake the builder's body in the grave." The windows rattled because the builder had not properly installed them. This incident deeply affected Sahiholnasab, reinforcing his commitment to doing even the smallest tasks correctly.

In Praise of Quality

The truth is, success is not a phenomenon unique to our time. According to Darren Hardy, even our grandparents and great-grandparents knew the rules of success, as did ancient humans. The rule is simple: work diligently, be consistent, and good things will follow. This means being committed to quality in your work. Quality itself is a significant advantage and can lead to business success. Quality is about centering your thoughts and beliefs around customer satisfaction. As John F. Akers, an American manager, said, quality begins when you place customer satisfaction at the core of your thinking. Another famous quote in this field states that quality is the opposite of chance; it is something achieved through thought and hard work. Another well-known saying is, "The consumer is our boss, quality is our job, and increasing profits is our goal." Of course, you don't need to focus on increasing profits because if you have the first two, the third will follow naturally.

Quality Means This:

The essence of quality in your work is to ensure customers return, not the product. Customers should be so satisfied with your product that they come back for more. This happened to Seyyed Hossein Sahiholnasab. In Argentina Square, Tehran, he built a complex called "Panj Dastgah." Interestingly, even after forty or fifty years, while surrounding buildings were frequently renovated or rebuilt, the one he constructed stood firm. Sahiholnasab recounts a day when someone recognized him on the street and asked, "Are you the famous Sahiholnasab?" When he confirmed, the person hugged him and expressed immense satisfaction with one of the apartments Sahiholnasab had built. Years later, this person's son sought out Sahiholnasab's children to buy another unit, saying, "Do you know who I am? I am the son of the man who hugged your father and thanked him." This is what quality does; it brings you success both in this world and the hereafter.

Staying Up-to-Date with Knowledge

Working in today's world is vastly different from working in the past. In today's world, you must acquire knowledge of your field, apply it to real-life experiences, and then enter your profession. For example, the accounting you learn in university differs from real-world accounting. You need time to align your academic knowledge with practical experience before starting your career. In Iranian business culture, there was a "master-apprentice" system, where you spent years learning from an expert before becoming a master yourself.

Knowledge, the Foundation of Business

In today's world, specialized knowledge is crucial for success. Without it, your progress will be slower. Young geniuses can now create knowledge-based startups with no limits to their progress, in terms of time, finances, production, etc. Jim Rohn notes that valuable achievements in life are placed on high shelves, and to reach them, you must stack books to elevate yourself. This metaphor emphasizes the importance of reading. Brian Tracy also stresses this point, suggesting that reading about your field for an hour daily can lead to reading about fifty books a year. This is significant, considering that a Ph.D. student typically reads twenty to thirty specialized books. Over ten years, this habit can make you an expert, much like how Warren Buffett reads eight hours a day, absorbing 500 pages, knowing that the more he learns, the better decisions he can make, which can lead to greater wealth.

The Importance of University Education

It is often mentioned that in Iran, many university majors lack good job prospects, and students should engage with the job market before graduation. However, fields like civil engineering, construction, architecture, and structural calculations require formal education. University education is necessary but not sufficient; you must continuously learn and study more about your field.

Importance of Up-to-Date Knowledge

Seyyed Hossein Sahiholnasab emphasizes the necessity of university education in his field, believing that without it, one will face difficulties. He even helps those who seek his advice and lack the budget for university, funding their education to ensure they become good architects or builders. In architecture and construction, you need both practical and theoretical knowledge. This dedication to modern practices and continuous learning has established the Sahiholnasab brand in construction. They stay current with global developments in construction and are willing to invest in the best materials. Consequently, their projects are highly sought after even before completion, and they receive many partnerships offers. Investors naturally prefer to invest in such a reputable brand, knowing their money will return with good profits. This success stems from their commitment to quality, knowledge, and continuous improvement.

The Real Effects of Parental Blessings

One of the important teachings in Eastern, especially Middle Eastern and Iranian business culture, is the respect for parents and elders. This might not be as prominent in Western business environments. However, in Eastern and Iranian businesses, there is a deep-rooted belief that having the blessings and well-wishes of parents and elders can lead to success. This doesn't mean that you can't achieve success without their blessings, but the success that comes with their approval tends to be more fulfilling and enduring. This belief hinges on the notion that if your parents or customers are pleased with you, God will be pleased too, showering you with blessings and easing the obstacles in your business.

Free Yourself

Although this perspective is common in the East, it can also be interpreted from a psychological viewpoint. A famous violin teacher claimed to make his students professional within a year, even though learning the violin typically takes five to ten years. Curious onlookers discovered that much of his teaching was psychological. He would ask his students to reconcile any disputes they had, seek forgiveness from their parents, and let go of past mistakes. After ten to twenty sessions of such exercises, the actual technical training would begin. With a cleared mind and a positive spirit, these students could rapidly master the violin. Essentially, they purified their minds and spirits before tackling technical challenges.

The Real Impact of a Blessing

Seyed Hossein Sahiholnasab is an example of someone who believes in the power of parental blessings. As a teenager, he worked hard, sending his earnings to his parents and keeping only what he earned in the evenings for himself. His mother's prayers, such as "May God make everything you touch turn to gold," stayed with him. This belief that divines support was with him helped him overcome obstacles. While some may question how a simple prayer can resolve issues, in our faith, we believe that God's power is the ultimate force in the universe. If God wills something, it happens effortlessly.

For those with weaker faith, this concept can still be explained. In the book "The Four Agreements," it is mentioned that humans are born free and capable of achieving anything. However, over time, societal and familial messages form agreements within us, dictating our limitations. For instance, if a child is repeatedly told they have a bad voice, they may grow up believing this and shy away from opportunities in singing or public speaking, missing out on their true potential.

A Message Embedded in the Subconscious

On the other hand, consider Sahiholnasab's mother continuously expressing her satisfaction and praying for his success. Such affirmations deeply penetrate his subconscious, forming new agreements that boost his confidence. He subconsciously believes that everything he touches will turn to gold, leading him to approach life with assurance. This positive mindset becomes evident to others, enhancing his chances of success. Essentially, his mother's prayers have set the stage for his achievements by fostering a strong, optimistic belief system.

In conclusion, the blessings and prayers of parents, from any perspective, have a profound and positive impact on an individual's success. Can we deny it?

www.ingramcontent.com/pod-product-compliance
Lightning Source LLC
Chambersburg PA
CBHW052206070526
44585CB00017B/2090